PRAISE

The urgency of *Confirm Humanity* grips us right from the very first page. The poems feel like walking a tightrope across the crevasse created by a maddening world and the dangers inherent in just being alive, while holding love as the balancing rod as you go. The world is complex and entangled with politics, memory, wildfire smoke, and ladybugs. But "the world awaiting us is the one right here," the author tells the evangelicals at her door, and we feel that, yes, this is exactly what we need to hear.

– Alice Major, author of *Welcome to the Anthropocene* and *Knife on Snow*

Filled with wit, warnings and lots of warmth, Kim Mannix's *Confirm Humanity* draws on science, social media, Saskatchewan, and past civilizations to contemplate wildfires, a miscarriage, the loss of a parent, motherhood, and the "end of everything." Kim's poems—rich with imagery and associative leaps—show how hope can be found in the "smallest affections," the memories picking berries, the lessons from ladybugs and octopuses, the healing of trees, a mother's navy cardigan, watching daughters on ice slides, enjoying "the best belly laugh," or in just waking up eager as "a girl in line for her first rollercoaster ride."

– Marco Melfi, author of *Routine Maintenance*

In Kim Mannix's poems, familiar alarms are sounded in a musical register, with intelligence, tenderness, and—yes, humanity. Mannix meets the current moment with a resonant anguish. Yet in memory, in motherhood, and in love, she also finds "something like wonder / sticking its bony finger in my fat dread." *Confirm Humanity* shows us that in the thick of grief or wildfire smoke, poetry is a lamplight to gather in.

– Jennifer Bowering Delisle, author of *Micrographia*

Confirm Humanity by Kim Mannix is that conversation with a dear friend you never want to end. Replete with reverie, reflection, wisdom, wondrous turns of phrase, and lines that beg to be read aloud, Mannix takes her reader on a journey through the ages of life, sharing stories from her own and her childrens' childhoods. Mannix is, at once, a daughter grieving her mother's death and a mother holding her daughter's hand to guide her across a crowded bridge. This book spans the wild and the tame, past and present, the scientific and prophetic, while inviting its reader to always consider what it means to be truly human. It a beautiful "reminder that all creatures are temporary." *Confirm Humanity* is an absolute delight, start to finish.

– Ellen Kartz, author of
Gravity: A series of I remembers

This is poetry that talks to you, tells stories; it's poetry of being-with, written in the key of empathy. If you'd like company as you chew over some of the Big Questions in the midst of your daily routines and personal ups and downs, *Confirm Humanity* can be that company. If you struggle with how to be hopeful, how to keep your chin up when decisions made by the powerful impose suffering, well, this book struggles too. Like Mannix's injured impala, who shows an impossible-seeming resilience, her poetry "writhes like a believer / with the gift of tongues."

– Sue Sinclair, author of
Almost Beauty: New and Selected Poems

Kim navigates life's challenges and tough subjects. She dives with a vulnerability into her own fears and with gentlest of voices soothes us that we aren't alone in our own fears and phobias. "…hold it in the darkness of your throat   speak butterflies." She challenges us to examine our own humanity and then confirms it.

– Daniel Poitras, author of the
forthcoming book *Frank Oliver Dreams of*
Amiskwacîwâskahikan

confirm humanity

POEMS

KIM MANNIX

© Kim Mannix

All rights reserved. No part of this publication may be reproduced, distributed, or transmitted in any form or by any means, including photocopying, recording, digital scanning, or other mechanical or electronic methods, without the prior written permission of the publisher, except in the case of brief quotations embodied in critical reviews and certain other non-commercial uses permitted by copyright law. For permission, please address Wild Skies Press.

Published 2025
Printed in Canada

ISBN Print 978-1-0693754-9-0
ISBN Ebook 978-1-997770-00-8

Cover Design by Alexis Marie Chute
Illustrations by Tetiana Lazunova, Vladim Rozov, and GaleartStudio
Interior Design by Alexis Marie Chute

For information address:
Wild Skies Press
A division of Alexis Marie Productions Inc.
Edmonton, Alberta, Canada
info@alexismariechute.com
www.WildSkiesPress.com

Wild Skies Press is an independent literary publisher founded in 2021. Wild Skies refers to the Aurora Borealis—northern lights—in Alberta, where the press is located, situated on Treaty 6 Territory. Wild Skies Press publishes non-fiction, fiction, poetry, and hybrid genres with an emphasis on the creation of Canadian works and books by emerging and established authors.
www.WildSkiesPress.com

for my mom

for my mom

Contents

Disturbing The Peace

- 15   Disturbing the Peace
- 16   We are not robots
- 17   Pigeon Domestication: A Guide for Billionaires
- 18   No Mishaps
- 19   No Ark
- 20   Octlantis
- 21   Patterns of Variation
- 22   As wildfires push the border
- 23   Countdown to Self-Destruct
- 24   Cliché, Cliché, Cliché
- 25   A belief of comfort
- 27   where to store hope

A Loveliness

- 31   Old Men Running
- 32   Memory, re-sequenced
- 33   Where are you at this moment in your life?
- 34   To see rust in a dream
- 35   The first shower after the miscarriage
- 36   You Won't Be
- 37   Somewhere Along the Coquihalla
- 38   At Eleven
- 39   A Loveliness
- 40   Alarm to Threat
- 42   Fine China
- 44   This tree is a goddess
- 45   Stranger Days
- 47   Forest Bathing When You're Dirty
- 48   Impala Rising

Something Like Safety

53 Fear of Water
54 Picking Saskatoons
56 While the Branches Fell
57 Ant Hills
58 Sister Memory
59 Yellowhead
60 At the Funeral Home
61 Accordion
63 Lessons in Bearing
65 What to Call It
66 There Will Be Gentle Things
67 Some Saturday With A Spirit Board
68 Trapping
69 Ghosts of Home
70 On the day we left
71 Awake
72 New Year's Eve
73 On Doomsday and Blue Jays
74 Through the Glass
75 Lightning
76 First Night in Jasper
77 I Ask My Therapist, Gaia, What It Means to Hold Space
78 definitions for a colour that is both blue & green
79 Simplicity
80 Watercolour

85 **Notes**
87 **Acknowledgements**
89 **Author Bio**

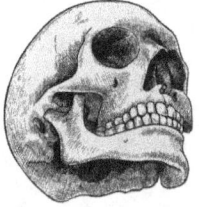

confirm humanity

POEMS

DISTURBING
THE PEACE

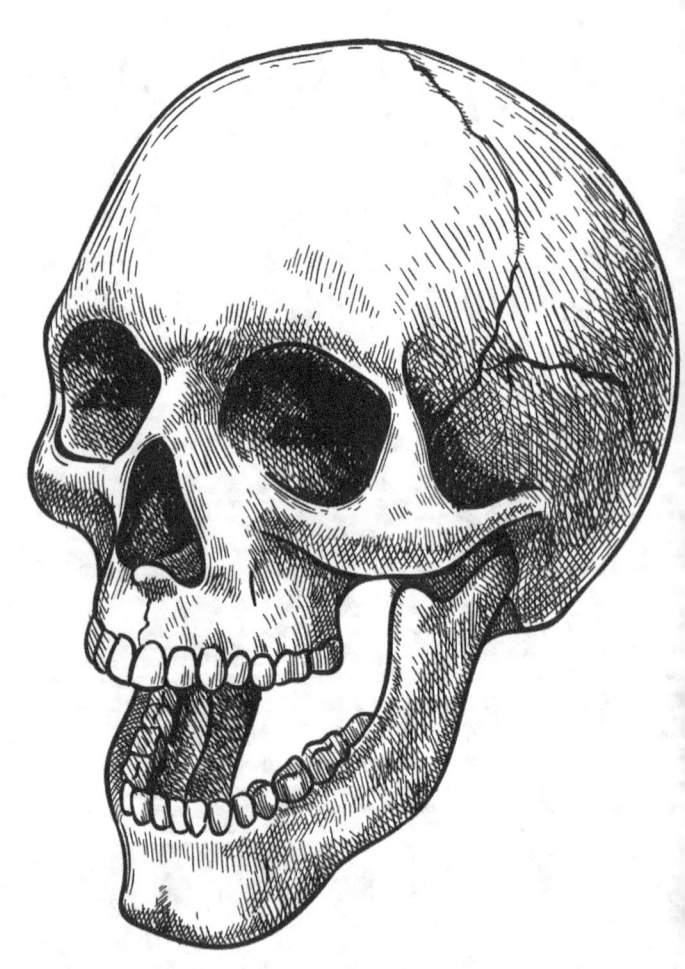

Disturbing the Peace

It's hard to keep your muscles loose, your teeth unclenched. Hard to hear the news over and over and over—insert city, number of dead here. Painting layer after layer of rage on top of you. It's a wonder you're not shellacked in place, fist up and mouth open, mid-anger shriek. How do you stay soft? How do you keep from popping your Ps on impossible words like prayer, peace, protection? How do you say you're a pacifist and mean it? It used to be so easy. Remember raising two fingers, like you saw the long-haired rock stars do on the covers of your dad's records? There's a plaque you still have in your living room, PEACE, LIKE CHARITY, BEGINS AT HOME. You've believed it for a long time. But lately you worry it ends there too. Praise, to all the brave souls, who still turn on the TV, refresh the newsfeed, open the front door, wave to a neighbour—their bodies as supple as a yogi's. Belief cushioning their red, red hearts.

We are not robots

Not yet. But Uncle had a pacemaker. When I was seven, I thought that meant he was good at keeping time. Asked him to count as I sprinted from his crumbling concrete steps to the door of the red barn. Third time was always the fastest. Before the Big Bang there was no space or time. I've read it in words even I can understand. Time comes faster the less we pay attention. Slips in unnoticed, like a silver inch of growth in your hair. Shimmery skin cells sealing a wound. Time advances no matter how much we crave pause. Space to breathe. Winds wail, then calm. Stars test the sky with the first pricks of light. Darkness readies. Click this space here. Confirm humanity.

Subscribe   to the notion we have control.

Pigeon Domestication: A Guide for Billionaires

As early as 10,000 years ago, it started. Peristeronic images on the tablets of Mesopotamia, in Egyptian hieroglyphics. Mentions of pigeon sacrifice in the testaments, old and new. Serving man's muscle, doing the dirty work, for longer than we've been bootlegging booze. Oil. Pills. Software.

There's a kind of lethargy to domestication. Taming takes patience. But it all starts with the cage. Line it with shreds of your most detested paperback. Keep a bin of treats nearby. Wait. Eventually the pigeons rely on you. It's ok to let them fly away. Illusions of security always bring them back.

Don't let the "sky rat" reputation scare you. The world's greatest have always been keepers. Darwin? A feather fancier. Gucci paid ten thousand for just one bird. England's royal lofts have been inhabited by pigeons since King Edward VII's reign. It's possible to build a throne from the bones.

Pigeon droppings can be toxic. Acidic as vinegar. Eroding stonework and metal. Entire bridges under threat of collapse from the weight and wear. It's hard to see just how fragile certain structures are until they're put under duress. But the carapace of wealth protects, and those with the most lose the least.

Eat the rich. Trending hashtag. And the dollars still climb in this unprecedented time. Raise a glass. Tonight's menu: squab served roasted with balsamic grilled eggplant. Get them young, supple. Most domesticated pigeons have been overworked. Their meat's gone sinewy.

No Mishaps

It's an ever-playing song, ironic and moronic, machine gun percussion, big rig motor grind, and Kid Rock as lead singer. But leaders, we know leaders. Leaders win and smile when we say, hey, it's a-ok, c'mon and drink the water with just an essence of lead. A danger? No danger, it's all in your head. Listen to your heart, listen to me, there is a war, but not that war—a war on freedom, a war on the good life, a war on you, it's just so very sad. And how dare they say cult? How dare they say fascist? They don't know the meaning, these very bad people. They will not clap for our glory. They will not stand. They will not cheer for our bigly achievements. No, they're feeding you lies between cosmic dread bread, but the answer is easy, the answer is here, no, NO, there's nothing under there, Look! OVER HERE! We make the sun shine, the sunshine is huge, a huge dose of Vitamin D, very important for good health, you take care of you, and we'll take care of us, but really, you'll thank us. It'll be amazing, you'll see. Did you taste the water? We have the best water, come swim in the water, no one drowns in the water, no one's forced into water. YOU, you are the one touched by migration, you are the one in need of safe crossing to the future of your past, to what came before and what came after. Remember? Do you remember, it was pure gold, our most perfect portrait in the tall shiny tower. Friends, you can be in that picture. You can be met with grace, the resurgence of everything great. Listen, do you hear it? That round of applause, the loudest hand claps from the biggest, best hands. That song that keeps playing, are you singing it now? Are you affected yet? Infected yet? They'll try to tell you that a vaccine exists, but the price is too high. The price isn't the sky, or the trees or the birds. The price is your life, they want you poor and sick, and we'll stop you from paying. We'll do you this favour. We'll give you the best. No mishaps, we're winning. We're good. We're so good. And yes, you should thank us. You're welcome.

No Ark

Snapshot. Tbilisi, Georgia. Floodwaters babble how myths are made. Once a zoo, now a macabre picture book, printed in murky browns. 300 animals dead, or drifting. See the round-eyed man cradle a limp and dirty bird. Watch the Samaritans pushing a lost hippopotamus back to his crumbled home. Stare at the mud-caked lion's once muscular body, sullied and ragged as a child's toy. Look now, just inches away, a grizzly bear splayed face down on the gritty street. Walls dissolved by the water rush—the animals flee. Perish. Survivors shucked from the sludge. Corralled again. Around the globe we watch. Click on the chaos. 21st century Noah collective, ruined.

Octlantis

At the bottom of a warm Australian bay, the octopuses build. They call it Octlantis, and if the reports are true, even Plato would approve. Clam and scallop shells, collected and moulded into shelter. A city of cephalopods, labouring side by side, communicating by changing colours. We're nothing if not curious, all the big-brained creatures. But it's the 'why' that evades the scientists, and me too. Long seen as the loner, do octopuses need? More than just shelter, safety—do they *need* each other? What if utopia is as easy as a construction project, a common goal? Linked arms, in arms, in arms.

Patterns of Variation

Firs know. Read caution in dry soil, the memory of petrichor. When a quench of rain comes, it shimmies up their roots. Sparkles in drops that dangle from their needles like earrings. A forest fiesta until the thirst of morning returns. Hangover in the weald, but silence is no cure. Can they taste it? The small changes, over seasons and years, drawing the facts in concentric circles. Autobiographies etched on their cores. Some patterns can only be seen close-up, under a microscopic lens. Some, plain sense—summer winds, roaring. Dragon flare, warning. Spectre smoke sending signals only the sky heeds. No cycle is eternal. No refuge is guaranteed.

As wildfires push the border

A sheet of smoke cloaks the sun. Coughs amber light onto the sidewalk. Suspicious robin sidesteps the beams, hops to the grass. Twilight feel at 9 a.m. It's the sky before vampires. Garbage truck headlights flick past the window. Moan of metal as it stretches an arm to snatch our waste. There was talk of swimming this morning, but the water can't be trusted. There's nothing to be done but shut the windows, close the drapes. Hand over the day to lamplight.

Countdown to Self-Destruct

Are there reasons to be hopeful? The clock's ticking. The omen's arrived. Tonight, after the ocean hushed, we listened for a siren in the distance. Listened between worried mutterings. Through the optimistic *Eureka!* of someone who thought they'd figured out how to bring back hope. *You're not listening hard enough,* they said. *Just put your ear here.* Held a purring cat to a microphone. Magic vibrations, 20 to 140 Hertz range. Power in the smallest affections.

There are reasons to be hopeful. At this moment a man in California is hearing his child laugh for the first time. Better, he's the one making the child laugh. A woman is being pulled from the Mediterranean Sea and will live. People are dancing in Helsinki. Someone's inventing new ways to be or not to be at all. Striking the slow burning match that sets off the self-destruct. The end of everything—but. Radioactivity subsides. Fauna revives. Flora grows. Winds blow. It lightens the heart, this natural resilience. Take a sip of tea. Dip your cookie. All goes on just fine without us.

Cliché, Cliché, Cliché

Like a lethal virus infecting a poem, we're all dead tired. Cliché, cliché, cliché—but the word itself sparkles on the tongue. Champagne fizz, French kiss, Brie de Meaux melt in my mouth, devour and hunger for more. I came to write about damage and here I am, delicious for trees again. Sky. Throw in a moon, a dove, and call it an elegy. Can I write a serenade to hope? Something something, hum a few notes, ablaze with light and a full heart. A sonnet for nature not stained by human hands. Can I describe a leaf without wearing right through a threadbare image? Can I branch away from setting down weapons, but still raise arms to touch clouds? Don't we all want roots anchoring us? There's a reason those of us who will, who try to, keep noticing the same things. Archive the same words. File away expired phrases. Repeat a saying like a song. Adage and adagio growing from the same source. We're all in need of a lullaby in the most familiar voice.

A belief of comfort

1.

Funny men have at least one sorrow story in their backpack. Heartbreak stuffed hastily in a pocket—the lover they won't talk about without looking down at their boots. A kindergarten pain they try not to remember until some strange Tuesday morning, when Def Leppard's "Pour Some Sugar On Me" comes on large between the weather and the traffic reports. Funny men are this way whether or not they try, reaching across a table to touch your hand when you can't stop laughing at their quip. They'll meet your eye, as if to say, *"Isn't it all such a weird fucking ride, babe?"*

2.

Isn't it all such a weird fucking ride, babe? A rock out there in space and all of us hanging on to something we don't even dare to name or talk about over breakfast anymore. Tea and toast are what Grandma said to take for the hurt that grates you. Gentle on the tummy. Warm in the mouth and tender, a bite with butter. Come now, let's sit at the table where it's still, less strange, so we might quell the motion sickness.

3.

Sickening how it keeps turning, not on a dime, but slowly. My daughter says sometimes at night she can feel the spinning behind her eyeballs. There are no retorts, at least no easy ones, to statements tossed like this. A bouncy ball against the brick wall of a school. Sometimes I remember the sound more than anything. Ka-chung ka-chung, a red rubber echo and the way my mom said don't turn down the far path behind the house. Oh, forbidden field. There are skunks there. A den that doesn't need the likes of you disquieting.

4.

Does one trauma overwrite another? When you make me laugh—best medicine, right? Cheaper than all those prescriptions—I wonder who you're covering for. Or if it's only for me. I sprout worry like dandelions, babe, but you're here. Weeding. I feel lonely sometimes, though these days we are never alone. Or we always are. I'm nagged more by what I'm supposed to feel than the actual feeling. You too. It's funny how much we're alike. In at least one sense of the word. Sometimes all we can do is stroke our own skins into a belief of comfort.

where to store hope

in caverns craving light   at the centre of a knot   where the shadow of one hand covers another   in the hollow of mother's collarbone   let it settle in the fissures of your skin   hold it   in the darkness of your throat   speak butterflies

A LOVELINESS

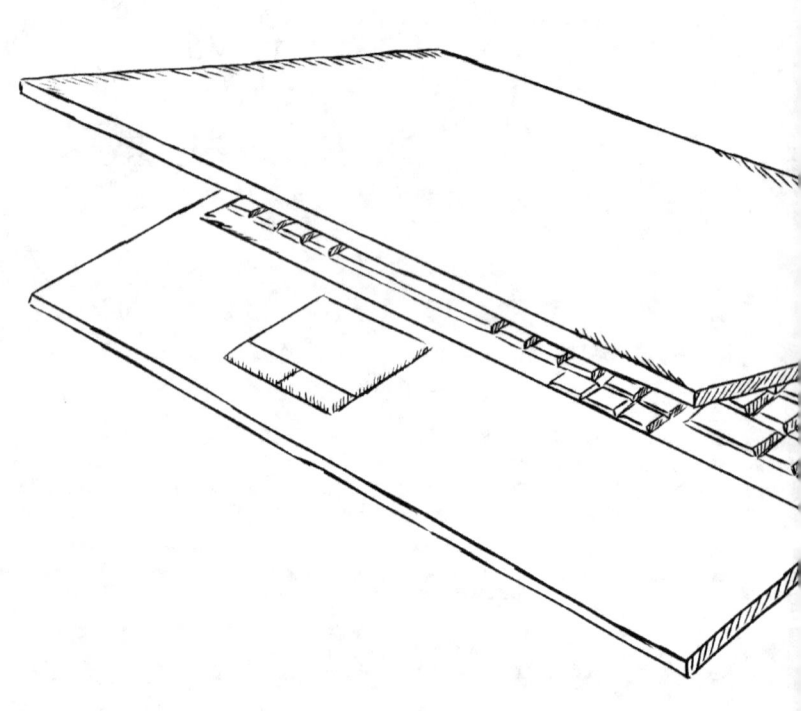

Old Men Running

Shadows from monkey bars draw
long black lines in the sand.
In the slightest wind, the swings sway.
Their chains groan and squeak
under the weight of nothing seen.

A flip-flop—hot pink, with daisies on the sole—
left by the merry-go-round, just a hint of
I Was Here. Two old men run,
in shorts and baggy t-shirts,
white socks pulled tight over sinewy calves.

When they run past you, they both turn, lips parting,
but instead of the *hellos* you're braced for,
grey moths fly from their mouths.
So many you can hear their wings thrumming.

Memory, re-sequenced

sparks
around the campfire
the shape of his jaw

a wood floor
the wetness
between the legs

two, four, six-pack
of girls prettier
than me

his hands
snapping
kindling

a mother
not mine
arrives

finally dark
at ten
moon shadows

fill me up, pour me out
only the shape inside
has changed

behind us
someone sings
an owl

Where are you at this moment in your life?

On Tuesday, I remembered drinking Malibu in the back
of your Camry and laughing until my ribs ached.
When was the last time I laughed like that?
I only thought about kissing you every time
we were together, and many times when we weren't.
I am 18, sometimes. I am 27.
Answering phones behind a desk
that felt like a slab of stone.
Do you ever put me in places I never was?
Swinging together at recess. Sitting with me
on the long bus ride after my dad nearly died.
Across the table at Starbucks while we talk about our kids.
Have you ever seen
Frida Kahlo's What the Water Gave Me?
The scar across the right big toe?
The strange and intricate renderings of life and death?
A maze of tendrils and shoots,
invading—the bathwater and perhaps her skin?
Sometimes you feel like this to me—a root, dormant.
I would be lying if I said I never Googled you.
You seem happy, but don't we all
in what we're willing to post.
I suppose, if I saw you at some concert,
or in the baking aisle at the grocery store,
I might ask you:

When does it stop being partly cloudy
and start to become partly sunny?
I might ask myself the same.

To see rust in a dream

is a warning. Aging, neglect—inevitable.
You are corroding. The quiver of fear you feel,
grating worry that your time has been misspent with
irrelevant men. It's gobbling you up.
Ripping you, like snaggled teeth,
tearing the pith from an orange.

You're your own worst judge, but sleep is honest.
A dream is never but a dream. In this one,
a line of women in hoods.
You can't see their faces, but their hands reach out,
wipe the sheen from your forehead.
Come here, to the half-full tub, they say.
Water, warm and clean.
You can leave possibility here, the almost-baby.
Rough draft. Meaning lost before being.

Your womb will be wide again.
Ready when you are, but hurry.
It's breaking down.
To see rust in a dream suggests
you are not reaching your potential.
Use it or lose it. One of these things will transpire.

The first shower after the miscarriage

You hated your body before you knew
it could disappoint you, but still use your favorite soap.
It will be ok the nurse said. A shampoo named Body Envy.
A man was responsible. But,
      the scent—orange; marigold; a freckled girl
      you wanted to kiss at 17—
      a woman made this.

You wipe a gash in the mirror steam.
He'll be there when the door opens. Okay.
It will be okay. In ten years,
      will the memory claw and snarl?
      Den itself someplace dim and warm?

Sometimes chance is a metallic tang on the lips.
Sometimes red flags are blood-soaked.

You Won't Be

There's no chance for innocence when your mother tries to safeguard you with stories about dead girls in car trunks. You won't be the one lured into a panelled station wagon with promises of ice cream, or stories of lost dogs, even if you feel guilty for not helping the search. You won't be the one who the other kids whisper about on the playground. *I heard he cut her into pieces and put her in the river. That's why they can't find her.* You won't be the one in black and white photo stasis, slapped on telephone poles all along First Avenue, wind torn edges and dark smudges where ink eyes have bled into something unrecognizable as child. You will be the one who walks up the driveway of a house that's not yours, pretending, pretending, pretending, until the slow-moving car has passed. You will be the one tapping the wall beside your bed four times before you sleep—one for every headline vanished girl. Some strange assurance that you won't be number five.

Somewhere Along the Coquihalla

Maybe this was the spot. Or this one. Highway lines blur into a long ribbon of yellow. We pass a rest stop and I wonder if it's a place she pulled into. Before.

Her car, late model Honda, grey like the stony mountaintops it was found next to. Contents—
    clothing;
    books;
    a small cooler with iced tea, a bag of baby carrots, homemade trail mix;
    purse left open on the passenger's seat.
    Driver's door ajar.

Probably suicide

    But she was excited about starting school

        I think it was a bear or cougar

Theories. Gossip. Best case scenarios.
Worst case scenarios not said aloud.

I keep hearing the officer…

    Nothing is ever really answered without a body…

We drive through a kilometer of dead trees. Landscape scars. Fresh undergrowth defying the blackened, bare branches above. Baby pines no taller than our toddler, asleep in the backseat. A curve in the road brings the sun to her face and I wish I'd put a towel in the window. To protect her.

At Eleven

Our heads are together and I can smell
citrus shampoo in her still-damp hair,
toothpaste on her breath when she says
I'm worried about growing up.
I know it's not just the body she inhabits,
the lengthening limbs and widening nose,
that brings this mental weight, but
the way the boy looked at her chest in gym class.
The man who called out while she rode her bike.
The principal's warning about the flasher in the park.

Things I have no explanation for.
Things I too feel the press of, and recognize
that at eleven, she already senses the
goodness of the world sullying,
the way a frenzy of expanding bubbles
start to pop and fade the minute the water
stops. Inevitable slide into something new,
that will contain so much greatness,
but also expose harsher truths. A body, a spirit,
asked to burden and endure, burden and endure.

I don't admit
that I, too, worry

All I have is
Shh, go to sleep
and some foolish faith that I'll find
the right words
      some morning
           or the next
           or the next.

A Loveliness

A moving mass
of ladybugs scarleted
the white wall
of my uncle's garage.

The entire south-facing side
afire
with spotted beetles.

It's a loveliness
he said.
They gather to hibernate.
He led me close enough to hear
the collective whirr
of thousands of lives
in congregation.

Gently, he touched his hand
to the wall, let the ladybugs run
across his skin, in and out
of his calloused fingers,
leaving yellow-orange trails.

Reflex bleeding, he told me. *It happens
when they're threatened.*
He shook his hand
and the ladybugs flitted up,
away, back to settle
in the throng.

That night I dreamt I had wings,
a ruby carapace,
a million sisters
to hold me
when I bleed orange.

Alarm to Threat

1.

More frog croak than coyote howl, nightly cry—*is anyone out there?* If I didn't think it'd wake the neighbours, I'd scream. Just to dislodge it from my throat, lonely lump of fear and anger. Clear night, brisk. On the deck I count stars. Cosmic census. Cold creeping through my socks, into my skin, permeating my heels. If I freeze in place like Ötzi the Iceman, who'll be here to find me in 5000 years?

2.

In my top kitchen cabinet, I store Mom's pitcher. The colour of milk, smooth. Looking at it is a comfort, yet I hide it. Well-kept, but still there's dust. I took it down for Easter brunch. Found a spool of red thread inside, needle thrust diagonally through. Did I put it there? This memory, another thing stored just out of reach.

3.

Accept the Past, Embrace the Future, Live in the Present. Wisdom of the dollar store Buddha, also jammed in the top cabinet. I endorsed the sentiment. Once upon a time. Believed the horn-shaped seashell I found on Long Beach might've been severed from a unicorn, too. Relic of a past, magical by nature of its distance from now. Reminder that all creatures are temporary.

4.

My daughter draws a frog. Green. Happy. I'm pulled back to biology class. *Lay the frog on its back, spread out its limbs, pin them to the tray. Make a small incision with a scalpel. Cut up the center of the body, being careful to slice through the skin only.*

All the facts scientific dissection omits. My frog was female.
Abdomen packed with black eggs. The resolve it takes just
to be born. The luck. When mating or raising alarm to
threat, some frogs call so loudly they can be heard a mile
away.

Fine China

The way into this poem is a hairline crack
from the lip of a white teacup, down, about halfway
where it intersects the petals of a painted yellow rose.

The way to go deeper is to think about
the woman who first bought this teacup—

not the auntie who gave it to you, with three others
that matched, the gold-rimmed teapot and four saucers
you leave stacked in the cupboard—

but the woman before that, a newlywed who ordered it
from a Sears catalogue or bought it with her third
paycheque when she worked
selling cigarettes and small talk.

You might've had a dream about this woman.
Or she might've had one about you,
at whatever age is considered prime.

You were shopping together, and when the salesclerk asked
What are you ladies looking for? you said, in unison
Funeral dresses.

Not our own, she added and you both erupted
in laughter. The sparkling, infectious kind
that shines a silence before it shatters.

Tea is better than coffee, for fragile bones
one of you said, so seriously,
before waking up from the dream.

The way out of this poem is to bring the teacup to your
mouth, sip from the spot where that crack begins.
Leave a scarlet lipstick stain on the rim.

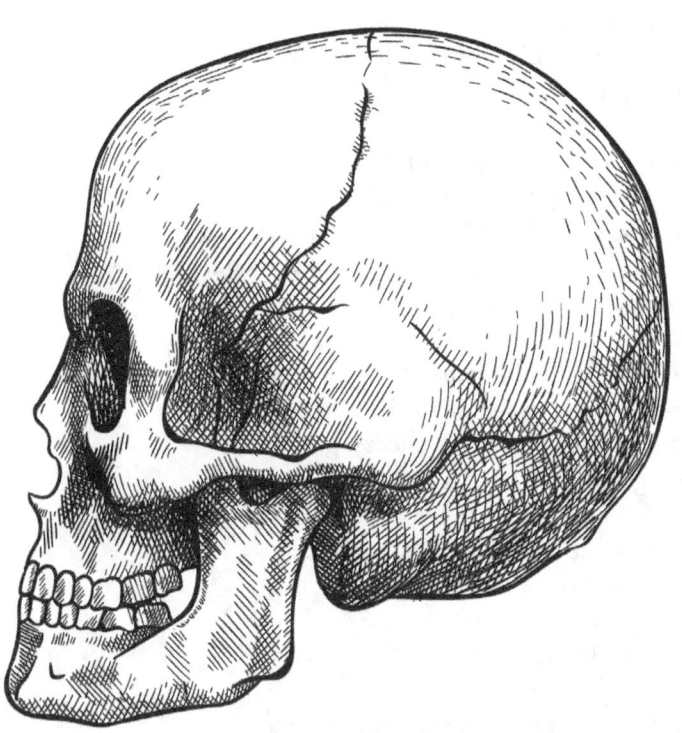

This tree is a goddess

Many-armed elder, stretched and reaching to light.
Enrobed in glory moss.
There are still things in this world
that can arrest me.

After a heart feared flattened
by the weight of worry. Life weary.
Pressed and dried like a leaf in a heavy book.
The kind of leaf this very goddess would cast down
in a breeze. Set at my feet.

Look! she would demand.
See how the veins grow from
midrib? An ordered intricacy, green
on green and

this is one of many off a branch,
sprung from a trunk,
in a verdant forest,
on this living rock.

Inhale and hold it like a prayer to me:
your problems are not so important, babe

Stranger Days

The newspaper ran a story about ten waitresses working at ten different restaurants who won the lottery this month, and five women on my block birthed healthy babies this week. The hares have multiplied. I counted twenty-five on my lawn this morning, and they've lost their fear of people. My daughter walked up to one, placed a red velvet ribbon around its neck, then leaned in close as if to hear it whispering. *She told me it's all part of the change, and soon we'll know*, my daughter said. Any other day I'd credit her imagination, but stranger days I do not recall. Every plant in my house bloomed overnight, and the air outside smelled of cinnamon. At the grocery store, every piece of fruit plump and unblemished. All the shoppers broke into "Good Vibrations," the harmonies perfect. I didn't even know I knew the words, but they knew me. And we sang ourselves out en masse to the parking lot, knowing just how long to hold the final note. A silver-haired woman began laughing when we finished, and I laughed too when I caught her soft brown eye. We all laughed for what felt like a year, but the sun never set. *Ahhh*, she sighed, like you do when you're spent from the best belly laugh. *Have you ever felt so happy? Is it the rapture? I don't know*, I replied, and I really didn't, but soon I was floating out of my shoes, unbuttoning my blouse, smiling as I flew up, up, up, with all the women, unencumbered.

Forest Bathing When You're Dirty

Because there are too many shadows in the trees
Carrie answers, keeping feet firm to the path
set here like a rule made mid-game.
Wildflowers I wish I could name
but in so doing they'd become tamer,
disappointing.
I thought I would find a solution here.
Which is not the same as an answer.

Someone has stuck a red push-pin
in the bark of a pine and I think of the flier
that might've been attached—*Live a trauma-free life*,
it would demand in ink, rain-pocked and faded, flapping
in the wind, fringed at the bottom with tearaway numbers
for a self-help class.
But help is inside out like a sweater chucked off
in frustration or passion,
hanging off the edge of an IKEA dresser.

Most mornings I want to wake up by a river
no matter how far or close you are to me.
Is this the problem, or the solution?
Carrie said a little nature would *do me good*,
which sounded salacious at the time.
Do me good, woods. Please. I'm begging.
There are birds speaking holy tongues
if I'm brave enough to accept
exaltation.

I ask Carrie why we can't wander a little farther
but her answer doesn't do anyone any good.

Impala Rising

In a video, I play and play again,
an impala is throat-crushed
then left limp by a leopard.
No sound, but palpable the gnash of teeth
on the creature's supple neck.
Lying in the scrubby grass,
eyes black and glossless
as the gratified leopard trots
to scare a duo of baboons.
The eyes of the camera, my eyes,
fixed on the flaccid animal,
moments ago springing, now a loose
gathering of bone, fur, horns.
In vigil, the spindly trees.

Like a pump has pushed
through her gaping mouth
round white belly inflates and falls.
Irregular at first, then with living rhythm.
Eyes blink and head lifts, shakes.
She writhes like a believer
with the gift of tongues.

Lady Lazarus of Kenya,
so numinous I wonder
if it should be seen.
Yet I witness again and again.
Fastened by my own disbelief.
Always the impala rises,
pulls herself onto four abiding legs,
lopes out of sight, to something like safety.

SOMETHING LIKE SAFETY

Fear of Water

At five, I watched *Jaws*
and no logic could convince me that sharks
didn't circle the shallows of our prairie lake.
A month later, my parents left me for a weekend away.
I played in the park with the babysitter
until the sky broke psychotic. Rain battered the city.
At home, our driveway a rising river, I quivered
in the babysitter's rusty hatchback
while water bled under the doors.
Grunting, she pried open the car door,
high water at her knees,
braved a smile, begging me to
come close, come closer sweetie,
but I anchored myself to the seat.
Wiggled my toes in my new pink sandals,
a gift from my mom before she left.
I kicked my legs and watched the sandals
drop into the cold puddle rising at my feet.
The babysitter was still coaxing
but all I heard was the rain, my breath, my panic.
Watching, waiting
for the monster's fin to break the surface.

Picking Saskatoons

We leave when there's a crack in the clouds.
Auntie gives me a windbreaker, bright orange,
smeared with dirt, loose on my ten-year-old frame.

We amble up the hill behind the house,
Auntie and Mom walking side-by-side through
ankle-high grass and scrubby weeds.
Mud dots the backs of their bare calves
with each step.

Oh! A deer! Mom says, points to a doe,
munching clover by a barbed wire fence.
Every lean muscle on the animal goes stiff.
*Better not tell the boys or they'll be out
with the rifle* Auntie says.
I wince, remember the red, meaty cubes
I've seen Uncle put in the grinder.

Just a half a click more Auntie says and smiles.
I knock the empty ice cream pail against my thigh,
think of how the thin metal handle will cut
into my palm on the way back,
when the pail's heavy with our labour.
We high step our way to saskatoon bushes,
short branches festooned with lush,
purple-blue berries.

Auntie and Mom chatter
as their quick hands pluck-pluck and plop-plop
the berries into their buckets.
I pull two matching clumps off the bush,
five berries on each, dangling like jewels.
Hold them up to my ears when Mom looks over,
to get a laugh.

Tempting, the fat ones,
when all the green's gone from the skin,
and you know if you pull too hard,
the ripe berry will squish between your fingers.

I pop one into my mouth,
press it against the back of my front teeth.
Say nothing when I feel a beetle skitter on my
tongue.

While the Branches Fell

Plow winds slammed the softball game at the bottom of the sixth. Came like all the best prairie storms, sudden and groaning. Winds tore elms from their roots, sheared the roofs from houses, tossed a McDonald's sign into the centre of our main drag. Us racing home. Smoke from my mom's anxious cigarette clouding the car. Dad, focused like a fighter pilot. Loverboy sang "Turn Me Loose." No one joined in. At home, we piled out and ran, Dad quick with the keys, holding back the door, waving us in. Me, stalled at the broken bottom step, peering under to see our tabby cowering, ears flat and eyes like burnished marbles.

Ant Hills

Each summer they seemed bigger,
spaced so evenly between the aspens on the lake road
that some magic or measure must have guided each colony.
Sandy monoliths, they looked, from our blue station wagon,
to be as tall as me. Maybe as tall as my dad and old, like
relics of a civilization born before the trees.

I never asked my dad to stop the car,
let me get close, let me watch the tiny red bodies shift,
climb, sculpt pine needles, dead leaves, rock specks,
into a home.

Safe and blurred behind glass,
I was content with my secret hope
that maybe I was the only one
who could see the mounds in the shadows.

Now, a cloudless December afternoon,
I hover by an ice slide, functional art carved in snow,
seeking my daughter's hot pink coat in the whirl of kids.
They clamor, slip, a clumsy mess of puffy limbs.
Chatter, screeches, carry them to the top where they stand,
eyes pinched against sun and cold.

At the front of the line, my daughter
crouching like a sprinter,
waiting for a smaller boy to clear the way.
She pushes off, glides down the white ice, boots first,
wincing or smiling, I can't tell.
A pause at the bottom to make sure I'm looking,
then she's up again—climbing with the swarm,
into the winter light.

Sister Memory

Take me there, down the hall, scent of home,
puff of lemon soap, cigarette smoke haze in my memory.

Each of us carries one, sometimes many, clenched in fists,
moulded by pressure, the shape of our memory.

My sister recalls an action scene, shot in black and white, a
drama I can't recall, or one I've scrubbed from my memory.

Another. Snipping baby's breath from a roadside, holding
bouquets too big for our hands, sun bleached memory.

One we need, smudged like a fingerprint, we recover with
dust. Using sharpened pencils to colour edges of memory.

Yellowhead

May was just lost. It crumbled into the shoulder
somewhere between Maidstone and Lloyd.
I watched it take three rolls
in the side view mirror before it turned to dust.
I put my hand on your forearm,
warm from the sun through the window.

We hoped for a coyote trotting in the ditch.
A hawk doing sky doughnuts,
gloating as he looped, while we forged straight.
Maybe a herd of roan cattle, all facing west.
We're too familiar with this road.

I wanted it to be the last time
we'd be here for awhile, heading back.
Going home, though I can say that no matter
which direction we follow this highway.
Past home, or present home.
The timeline's gone slack. This will be our summer.
Back and forth trips to check up.
Spend just a few more hours with her
while I can.
Birthdays at my old house.
Some belief that reverie
can stall the foreseeable.

Drone of tires on rutted asphalt bores into our skulls.
We look forward to our bed, though I left it unmade.
I'll leave our bags mostly packed.
The clothes will keep.
And it will be one less thing
to do in case the next trip is sudden.
In case it's the last.

At the Funeral Home

My sister takes the invitation
to view Mom's body,
painless now, serene,
in this place where they know
the business of death;
the management of the living.

I don't go. I already know
that her soft grey hair,
the gentle slope of her nose,
her hard-worn hands will be
familiar as ever, but
what's left is not what she was.

But I know too, why my sister goes.
What she needs to find in the room.

It's like there's a gate unlatched
squeaking in the breeze.

If you didn't see her go,
you'll keep expecting
her to stroll back, barefoot,

push the gate until it clicks.
Wave to you from the other side.

Accordion

You hear it again. Drone from a dark hall.
A drawn-out note, weary of its own dread.
Dead mother song
looped. Like the way a year
spins into the next, then more.

You are somewhere reading this now,
writing this, dreaming this. You are also some-when.
Memory a time traveller you can latch onto
for relief—

tasting the first raspberry
at Grandma's house, hot July

brushing the feathery down
on your baby's head—

Unhook
from greyer thoughts.

Mother mouth opening closing opening,
a panicking trout on the floor of a boat.
Breath, a privilege you never considered
until you watched hers disappear.

The bellows of an accordion
are made of paper. Blank,
until the air gives them meaning.

In the dream
you are mistress of the squeezebox.
Expanding, contracting,
writing a concord of sound.
Clavicle alive with hum.

Stitch that feeling
into the very heart
of you. Melodeon
memory, mourn.
You cannot compress
until you release.

Lessons in Bearing

1.

You haunt me in unexpected ways. The shamrock plant you gave me, withered a year before you did. Revival a year later in a silver pot forgotten on the sill. I pass an older woman, scent of lilies and cigarette smoke. I imagine asking for a hug, inhaling deep, expecting to feel home in a stranger's embrace. You've appeared in my daughter's eyes, open wide and bright. When I tell her about a moment with you—one I'm scared of losing—she grabs my hand. Already the knowledge that ghosts are too heavy to carry alone.

2.

When I was young, you ruled this house like a weather system. Quick bluster, thick air, warm light and a hint of ozone after some argument had cleared. Now an unchanging quiet. So much stillness, I hear the gentle sound of a dead leaf from the money tree falling to the floor. Anger can make things easier. Burn up what's held too long. How neatly I folded each sweater, your many sets of flannel pajamas, only to stuff them slapdash in black garbage bags. Even when we try not to, we always leave something of ourselves behind. Your peach lipstick, worn to a flat nub. Whiff of coconut shampoo on the hair wound in your brush. Your box of crochet hooks, sorted by colour and size. I remember watching you loop and turn, creative sleight of hand, hats, sweaters, blankets conjured like magic. Or the way you'd curse at a stitch gone wrong, pulling back rows and rows with frustrated fingers, twisted strands of white yarn puffed around your feet like a cloud.

3.

My girls, who don't remember you, speak of you as though you're away on a trip. Close, the way the scent of a houseguest lingers on the sheets they slept on. I believed in angels for a time. When I needed to. What little girl wouldn't shut her eyes and imagine wings? Sorrow is stone carried in the chest. No one needs breath in heaven. If there is a there, you walk barefoot through the grass. Tend a garden. Know all the names and reasons for the flowers you grow. Pluck petals and cast them below   loveme loveme   loveme   not is a finite word. If you can see me, you already know I've planted irises. Mustered all the faith I can believing they'll bloom.

What To Call It

Before there were apps
how did anyone know what to call
the errant purple bloom
cloaked in spruce's shadow?
Did it whisper its name
to the first human who tried to
snap its stem? Does it
need a name at all?
Can it flourish, identify
by the brush of a tiger moth
against its petals?

If I wanted to describe this flower
to my mom, mine her wisdom through
a collect call to the clouds or sunbeams or birdsong
or whatever expanse she fills today,
where would I start?

By explaining the leaves, tiny and saw-toothed?
Its prep-school posture, stalk not even bending to
the morning light? Speak of a colour
like the violet swatch in sometimes sunsets?
Just a shade lighter than grief.

There Will Be Gentle Things

I miss normal she whispered, as I traced
a circle across her back, some kind of
dial to move her toward sleep,
to a quieter place than this darkened bedroom,
where the hard edges and jagged ridges
of the last year have dissolved into
soft S sounds, the small swish
of two pages closing against one another.

Some Saturday With A Spirit Board

My daughter finds the Ouija board between the Monopoly
box and a poker set.
Hasbro brand, because even ghosts can be sold.
Who should we contact? she asks, smiling
and I think of the small semantic difference between séance
and science.

I don't need a planchette to lead me to you. There are
always dreams,
strange and funny. Absurdity is a good balm. Or the ones
where we're together again as you die. Those days
sorrow stays like a sore muscle after a workout.

I play along, pretend it's not she or me nudging
the pointer toward YES.
YES you are there.
YES you are here.
YES you see us.
YES you are happy.
YES you've noticed I'm wearing your old navy cardigan
There's a hole in the sleeve, I'm sorry, and
NO it wasn't a moth,
just how time wears away at things.

Trapping

I'm drinking coffee with Dad in his kitchen,
when he tells me how he used to trap skunks
and collect coins for their pelts.
Boyhood entrepreneurship
in his rural Manitoba youth.

He'd wait for days.
Made sure the skunks starved,
or froze, before he returned.
He didn't have the stomach
to do them in himself.

I'm shocked, then queasy, at the brutality.
So unlike the gentle man I know.
Yet completely him all the same.
Needing those little deaths,
but too soft-hearted to witness.

Ghosts of Home

We were warned at nineteen that home will always haunt us. We tucked the notion in our pockets along with our parents' worries and headed East to begin. The ghosts we kept stretched long inside us, threatening to break open the circuitry of concrete cities. Eager at twenty-five to forget how long a voice roars through miles of open space. But we couldn't be held back from the whitest of winters, when even midnight gleams. All that shrouded land shrieking light into the night. We were stirred not by the stars, but the hollows between them. We fell flat backed in cold fields, noses to the sky, hanging on every phase of the moon.

On the day we left

the apartment
we'd worn like a ratty sweater
for five years of couplehood,
we took with us
two cats who'd made it a home;
a baby, who'd made it too small
and the futon she'd been conceived on.

Left: dirty windows,
an old desk too big for the van
and our belief that
we couldn't ever be happier
than we were then.

Awake

If dawn is a rebirth, have I been dead all night? Soul-sucked with a cosmic vacuum hose, then spit back out by sunrise. Today reanimation came with confusion. I smelled lilacs. Heard chickadees. Thought it was the July we spent squatting in my Auntie Anne's cottage. Sliced sunlight came through the blinds, striping you like a zebra. But it's the long end of a cold spring. You were so still that I put my hand to your chest to be sure you were breathing. *Nous vivons, ma chère,* but it will happen that way. Someday. Maybe not in our bed. Maybe not in a hospital. Maybe not in a car accident. Maybe not in a plane crash. But someplace where everything is white: snow sky snow flies snow covers it all. To witness death is the surest way to feel alive. Some days I wake up so eager, I'm a girl in line for her first rollercoaster ride. It's a new day! I believe in the colour yellow. Pan made his pipe from hollow cane rods. I can hear it now. Can you? Feel the shrill notes brushing my cheeks while I fly above the yard, circling like a vulture. When the birds feed together, backs hunched over a carcass, the group is called a wake.

New Year's Eve

It's a slow retreat across the wooden footbridge,
all of us purged of excitement, spent
like the shower of sparks that poured down on the night.
The air holds a chill, but no hard winter for weeks,
and a boy, maybe eight, spins his toque
on the end of a plastic lightsaber.
A man's elbow presses my side,
a woman's frizzy hair grazes my mouth.
I want to pick up my daughter, but she's six
and there's no room to hoist her up,
out of the crushing crowd. We're stalled, for a beat,
at the apex of this tiny bridge
dangling over the ice-skinned creek.
*If this thing were going to collapse,
now would be the time*, says a red-haired woman,
smiling at her husband. My daughter hears
and squeezes my hand, tighter through our fleece mitts.
I bend as much as the dense pack of people will allow
and say softly into her ear, *we're almost across.*

An hour later, in her bed, her eyes drooping
after the long night, she asks how we know
when the New Year starts.
It's just a day on a calendar, I tell her.
A year has to start and end somewhere.
I start to explain twelve months, fifty-two weeks,
say I don't know if it's Gregorian or Julian—
but someone, sometime
saw the need to carve a notch into a constant circle—
but she's asleep.
For a long time, I'm still.
Listening to her deep, even breaths.
A quiet metronome, setting the pace
for wherever we're going.

On Doomsday and Blue Jays

The doomsdayers at my door greet me in sensible skirts and shining, foundjesus smiles that falter when I can't agree that the world is getting worse. *Isn't life easier once we know there's a loving heaven waiting for us?* Oh, ladies, ladies, look over there. See that blue jay jeering in the evergreen? I've heard they partner for life, encourage curiosity in their chicks, and can fly as fast as my grandpa used to drive his gleaming New Yorker down the gravel road. (That is to say, fast enough to get on with things, but not so fast that he'd cause a stone chip). When I was a kid, a young jay couple built a practice nest on top of our yard light. They were like family to my mom, taking peanuts mere inches from her still feet and, she hoped, maybe one day right from her hand. I wondered about the peanuts—how was it that a bird so at home in the prairies came to love a warm-climate legume that sprouts in the loamy underground? Who gave the jay its first taste, hard shell offered up in an open palm?

I'm a cynic most days, but I know my place. The world awaiting us is the one right here—one where even birds know nothing's built right the first time. Now, if I may ask you ladies, is it a relief to learn that the blue jay isn't blue at all? Its colour comes from the feather structure, a wondrous trick of refracting light. And does it really matter that when you crush them between your fingers, the feathers turn brown?

Through the Glass

January view, again,
which never seemed like much of anything before.

Lilac bushes, heavy with mauve throughout the summer,
now black branches backlit
by sunrise hues of pink and orange.

I linger at the window, half-expecting the hare
who mirrors season's change,
to look up at me, eye meeting eye.

Magpies, so common their calls that I hear them as kin,
with need, with warning.

The progression of flowers, from seed to sprout,
blossom and regress.

My dread that the bleeding-heart bush won't last
the winter.

This is a grounding experience
        I whisper to myself on the hardest days.
        But another meaning of grounded
        is to be fixed. Trapped. Pinned,
        like a butterfly mounted under glass.
        How jarring the wings, splayed.
        Tissue-thin. Perpetually immobile.
        How strange what we keep for later beauty's sake.

Lightning

Out there, squares of prairie butt up against one another. Bordered by roads, wire fences, knurly lines of pine planted by men with meaty palms and sun basted forearms. In shadow rest now, thick July night draped over fields of wheat, canola, flax, like the heaviest quilt in Grandma's hall closet. Our girls are asleep in the backseat, heads bent at angles that make my neck ache. They dream through a low grumble of thunder. A forked flash jolts us from the trance of a long drive, lights the road ahead.

A switch flicks in a dim hall of memory. Another summer, another heavy night. You're asleep on the bed. I wear only your t-shirt as I step onto the balcony, count the lit windows of other apartments decorating the cityscape like a glow-in-the-dark mosaic. I smell cooking onions, from someone else's open window, and a suggestion of shampoo, yours or mine, cedar and peppermint. Lightning makes everything day, for less than a moment, afterimage scorched on the eye. What a cliché to have an epiphany now, but that's not exactly the right word. More like an affirmation. An idea we've both been holding. There's no one I'd rather ride out a storm with than you.

First Night in Jasper

This is a new dark
and though I prepared for stars,
I'm still caught with something like wonder
sticking its bony finger in my fat dread.

It's like a pocket place you said about the campsite,
just this afternoon, pulling sleeping bags
from the back of the car. I looked all
the way up, to where the trees jabbed
the sky. Almost forgot the hollowness
we left five hours back.

I didn't hear it then, but the river thrums,
even this far from the edge. Like darkness
cups the sound, forces us to take turns
holding it. Maybe from now on.

I Ask My Therapist, Gaia, What It Means to Hold Space

Imagine the dimple in the river's edge when you pluck a stone for your pocket, the way water embraces the vacancy.

Listen to the robin sing, but attend more deeply to the silence that cradles the notes.

When the forest huffs, trying to catch its breath, notice how the grey clouds bustle in, alert to thirst.

Relish the sweetness of the most sincere strawberry, how it blushes your fingertips with a keepsake kiss.

Be.

Trace the indigo veins on your wrist to mimic the whorls and loops of your grandmother's handwriting.

If a golden wheat stem bends its head toward you, donate your ears, your heart without expectation.

definitions for a colour that is both blue & green

waking sighs

>   the shape of your tongue when you say the word *visceral*

speckle of sweat on your mother's forehead

>   school hallways at night

>   >   cold fingers

a dress you wore in Friday night's dream

>   shoe screech on polished floor

soap slipping from your wet hand

>   kids laughing as they log roll down a hill

pressing on a bruise

>   the difference between mumble and murmur

a glacier, calving

>   the first person you think of when it's raining

Simplicity

My six-year-old daughter tells me how it is:
you meet, kiss, get married, have babies if you want,
but it's ok to not want them too.

At her age, it's easy to spot the bad guys:
Their voices sound meaner, they wear masks,
or have bad laughs and their music is scarier.

At bedtime, like a prayer, she names all the people she loves,
then all the people who love her back.
The lists are the same.

She presses her head into her polka-dotted pillow,
wriggles her body until she's comfortable and still.
The whole world is small and soft, like a stuffed lamb.

Watercolour

She asks why the water's blue.
I tilt her chin to the sky, try to clarify specular reflection
in a way that's more concrete than mirrors.
Offer a purely chemical answer: pollution, kiddo

Later, I read the colour is intrinsic. Is as it is.
Blueness created when wild molecules dance to light.

Had I known, then, I never could've explained.
Watching her kneeling on the rocks,
slapping her hands at the place where sea meets land.
No way to parse the science from the marvel.

Just her, dabbed like a pink brushstroke on a backdrop
of blue, blue water and boundless sky.

Notes

- "Disturbing the Peace" appeared in Issue 9 of *These Days* zine
- "where to store hope" was published in *Reimagining Fire: the Future of Energy* and in various gallery exhibits as part of the Energy Futures Project, edited and curated by Eveline Kolijn and inspired by artwork by Jamie-Lee Girodat
- "Where are you at this moment in your life?" was published in *Capital City Press Anthology: Volume V*
- A version of "Memory, re-sequenced" was published in *Resistance: Righteous Rage in the Age of #MeToo*, edited by Sue Goyette
- "Alarm to Threat" and "definitions for a colour that is both blue & green" both appeared in *Poetry Pause* by the League of Canadian Poets
- "Stranger Days" was published in *FreeFall Magazine*, Volume XXIX Number 1
- "Forest Bathing When You're Dirty" and "First Night in Jasper" appeared in *Identity Theory*
- "Sister Memory" was printed in The Stroll of Poets anthology, 2018
- "There Will Be Gentle Things" won the Ontario Poetry Society's 2021 Ultra Short Poetry Competition and appeared in their *Ultra Best Short Verse Anthology*
- "Ghosts of Home" appeared in *Gnarled Oak* and was nominated for the *Pushcart Prize*
- "Awake" was published in *Savant-Garde*, Issue 6
- "On Doomsday and Blue Jays" appeared in r*elease any words stuck inside of you II: Canadian Flash Fiction and Prose Poetry*, edited by Nicole Haldoupis and Geoff Pevlin

Acknowledgements

So many have helped this long labour of love take shape. First, I express gratitude for this beautiful Earth and for the places that have and do sustain me, physically and spiritually. Thanks to writer and friend Laurel Sproule, for her conversation, insight and empathetic heart. Thank you to the many mentors, writers-in-residence and wise wordsmiths I've consulted over the years, especially Sue Sinclair, Alice Major, Jannie Edwards, Rayanne Haines, and Margaret Macpherson. Thank you to the Writers' Guild of Alberta, Stroll of Poets Society, Parkland Poets, and League of Canadian Poets for all you've done for me and for poetry in general. Thank you to everyone at the Edmonton Poetry Festival, which is not just a society, but a family. Gratitude to Daniel Poitras for reading my work with a keen eye and a poet's soul. I'm grateful to Alexis Marie Chute and Fiona Pearson at Wild Skies Press for helping to make this book a reality. Thank you to the most inspiring teacher ever, Paul Jacoby. Thank you to my many friends and cheerleaders—new and old—all across Canada, in cities I love and miss. A giant thank-you to my family, especially my in-laws and my sister, brother, and dad. Thanks for being the coolest, always. And to my mom for inspiring me even still. Finally, eternal love and gratitude to my amazing husband and two beautiful kids.

KIM MANNIX

Author Bio

Kim Mannix (she/her) is a journalist, poet, and short fiction writer who lives and creates on Treaty Six territory in Sherwood Park, Alberta.

Born and raised in Saskatoon, she is a graduate of both the University of Saskatchewan and the University of Regina and has lived and worked across Canada. Her passion for climate justice issues, the importance of art, feminism, and parenthood intersect in both her creative and professional pursuits.

Mannix is a contributing editor of *Watch Your Head*, a climate crisis anthology, and a freelance entertainment and lifestyle writer. She currently serves as President of the Edmonton Poetry Festival and is an avid believer that everyone, everywhere, has a little poetry in their soul.

Her poetry and prose have appeared in numerous Canadian and American journals and anthologies. *Confirm Humanity* is her first book of poetry.

Other Books from Wild Skies Press

www.WildSkiesPress.com

www.ingramcontent.com/pod-product-compliance
Lightning Source LLC
Chambersburg PA
CBHW050330010526
44119CB00050B/735